Trip to Guava Farm

By Nimo Mohamed
Hobaan Books – where imagination is fostered

Dedication

For Ila, Hibo-Yar, and Zeinah

One early summer morning, Essa and Hawa and their two kids, Ayan and Abbi, took a trip to Farmer Farah's guava farm. The family set out on foot to get to the farm. They took the largest dusty road in Somaliland, in the Horn of Africa to get there.

"Let's take the dusty road to the farm." said Hawa. "This is the guava harvest season. We'll have large guavas for lunch. The guavas will be ripe and delicious."

Farmer Farah grew guavas, limes, oranges, grapefruits, mangos, pineapples, bananas, pomegranates and papayas. He had goats, donkeys, a bull, and chickens on his farm.

"Let's take the dusty road to the farm." said Hawa. "This is the guava harvest season. We'll have large guavas for lunch. The guavas will be ripe and delicious."

"Papa, Mama, and Abbi look out for the ants marching to cross the road," said Ayan on their way to the farm.

"The ants wanted to get to the fruit trees on Farah's Farm," laughed Abbi.

"No, children. Their home was probably destroyed by careless loggers and they are moving to another place. Look, they are carrying their eggs in their mouths," said Papa.

"What kind of ants are they, Papa?" asked Ayan.

"Orange coloured, sweet-loving ants. You probably have seen them looking for sugar in our yard occasionally," answered Papa.

"How do we pass them?" asked the children.

"We cannot step on them. We cannot pick them up. We will not scare them. We cannot wait to let them pass. We must step over them," directed Mama.

"Let's take the dusty road to the farm. This is the guava harvest season. We'll have large guavas for lunch. The guavas will be ripe and delicious," said Hawa.

"Look, Farah's four chickens crossed the road and want to feast on the ants!" said Papa.

"How do we pass them?" asked the children.

"We cannot step over them. We cannot step on them. We cannot scare them. We cannot wait to let them pass. We will take them with us to Farah's Farm," answered Mama and Papa, laughing.

"Let's take the dusty road to the farm. This is the guava harvest season. We'll have large guavas for lunch. The guavas will be ripe and delicious," said Hawa.

They all ran to catch the four chickens.

"Catch it, Abbi. Don't let it pass you!" shouted Ayan.

Abbi caught the first chicken, then Ayan caught the second chicken. Ayan and Abbi watched and laughed at their parents struggling with the other two chickens.

"Let's take the dusty road to the farm. This is the guava harvest season. We'll have large guavas for lunch. The guavas will be ripe and delicious," said Hawa , still chuckling and holding one chicken against her chest.

"Look, a scorpion chasing the ants now," said Mama.

"How do we pass it?" asked the children.

"We cannot pick it up. We cannot step over it. We cannot wait to let it pass. We will not scare it. I will step on the nasty scorpion and crush it to save the ants and their eggs," declared Papa.

"Let's take the dusty road to the farm. This is the guava harvest season. We'll have large guavas for lunch. The guavas will be ripe and delicious," said Hawa, still chuckling and holding one chicken against her chest.

"Look at the tall anthill blocking the road," said Ayan.

"How do we pass it?" asked Abbi.

"We cannot step on it. We cannot pick it up. We cannot scare it. We cannot step over it. We must climb over it," answered Papa.

"Let's take the dusty road to the farm. This is the guava harvest season. We'll have large guavas for lunch. The guavas will be ripe and delicious," said Hawa.

"Wait, let us get out of the way!" shouted Papa.

But the kids scrambled over the anthill, and quickly got to the top, and looked down.

"Oops! Papa and Mama were covered with dust and sand was pooled at their feet.

"Sorry, Papa. Sorry, Mama," said the kids sheepishly.

"Let's take the dusty road to the farm. This is the guava harvest season. We'll have large guavas for lunch. The guavas will be ripe and delicious," said Hawa who was now dusty, sweaty and breathing hard.

"Look, a cactus tree with purple flower and red fruits," said Abbi.

"Can we get the fruit? How do we pass it?" asked the children.

"We cannot step on it. We cannot go over it. We cannot pick it up. We must go around it," answered Papa.

"Cactus fruit has thorns, but we could get the fruit with gloves."

"No spoiling your appetite! Let's take the dusty road to the farm. This is the guava harvest season. We'll have large guavas for lunch. The guavas will be ripe and delicious," said Hawa.

"Can you see the herd of camels crossing the road to the market?" "They will be shipped to other countries to be sold," said Mama.

"Can we buy milk from them," pleaded Ayan.

"How do we pass them?" asked Abbi.

"No milk, only male camels are exported," explained Mama.

"We cannot step on them. We cannot pick them up. We shouldn't scare them. We cannot go over them. We cannot go around them. We must wait for them to pass," added Papa.

"Let's take the dusty road to the farm. This is the guava harvest season. We'll have large guavas for lunch. The guavas will be ripe and delicious," said Hawa.

"Look, children. That is Farah's bull for his farm," said Papa.

"How do we pass it?" asked the children, now bored.

"We cannot step on it. We cannot pick it up. We shouldn't scare it. We cannot climb over it. We cannot wait for it to pass. We must steer it back to the farm," replied Papa.

The kids ran after the bull. "shoo, shoo," they shouted energized and laughing. Essa and Hawa joined them and help steer the bull toward the farm.

"Let's take the dusty road to the farm. This is the guava harvest season. We'll have large guavas for lunch. The guavas will be ripe and delicious," said Hawa, feeling victorious and walking behind the bull.

"Look! Two women are carrying bundles of clothes on their head," said Abbi.

"What are they doing? How do we pass them?" asked Ayan.

"They are taking the clothes to the river to wash," replied Mama.

"We cannot pick them up. We will not scare them. We cannot go over them. We must walk beside them on the road," replied Papa.

"Can we help you carry the clothes?" asked the kids.

"No, thank you," replied the women, smiling at them.

"Let's take the dusty road to the Farm. This is the guava harvest season. We'll have large guavas for lunch. The guavas will be ripe and delicious," said Hawa.

"Do you see the donkey with a cart full of bananas?" noted Ayan pointing.

"I see it, but how do we pass it?" asked Abbi.

"We cannot pick it up. We will not scare it. We cannot go over it. We cannot wait for it to pass. I don't know," replied Papa.

"That is Farah's donkey cart. Ask the driver to take you to the farm," suggested one of the women who was carrying the clothes.

Essa asked the driver, and they got a ride on the cart.

"Let's take the dusty road to the farm. This is the guava harvest season. We'll have large guavas for lunch. The guavas will be ripe and delicious," said Hawa.

Suddenly the donkey farted, and started braying, "Hee-haw, hee-haw!"

Sitting on the back of the banana cart, the kids screamed, jumped from the cart, and ran across a little bridge over the river right into farmer Farah's Farm.

"That was awful," they laughed, holding their hands over their noses.

Their parents and the donkey driver laughed and crossed the small bridge over the river on the banana cart into Farah's Farm.

"What is this?" asked Abbi. He noticed a wasps' hive hanging from an old tree and poked it with a stick.

"Don't touch!" shouted Farmer Farah, running toward them. But it was too late. Out came the angry wasps, buzzing.

"Run, run! The wasps are disturbed and angry," shouted Farmer Farah. The whole family ran back to the river and jumped in. The wasps passed over them. The parents and kids came out wet and laughing. They sat near the river to dry.

Farmer Farah came with four baskets of guavas, papayas, mangoes and oranges. They sat down for a picnic and ate it all, laughing throughout the lunch. The guavas were delicious!

"How was your trip?" Farmer Farah asked the children.

"We chased, and picked up your chickens. We stepped on the scorpion to save the ants. We climbed on the top of the anthill."

"We walked around the cactus tree, but didn't get the fruit. We brought your bull back to the farm. We hitched a ride on your donkey cart, but it farted at us."

"We were able to hide from the angry wasps. We had the best picnic by the river, and the guavas were delicious. We had a fun trip!" replied the children, laughing.

"Wow! That sounds like a great trip," said Farmer Farah.

"Yes, it was, and we loved it," said both kids, still giggling.

"How about if I drive you home in my pick-up truck? But only if your father agrees to ride in the back with the sheep for sale," said Farmer Farah, laughing along with them.

"Hooray!" shouted the kids. They were excited and ready to go home.